The History of Medicine

Medicine in the Middle Ages

Ian Dawson

ENCHANTED LION BOOKS
New York

OCT 0 2 2006

First American edition published in 2005 by
Enchanted Lion Books,
115 West 18 Street,
New York, NY 10011

© Hodder Wayland 2005

Commissioning editor: Victoria Brooker
Editor: Deborah Fox
Inside design: Peta Morey
Cover design: Hodder Wayland
Picture research: Shelley Noronha, Glass Onion Pictures
Consultant: Dr Robert Arnott, University of Birmingham Medical School

Library of Congress Cataloging-in-Publication Data

Dawson, Ian.
  Medicine in the middle ages / Ian Dawson.—1st American ed.
      p. cm.—(History of medicine)
  Includes bibliographical references and index.
  ISBN 1-59270-037-3
  1. Medicine, Medieval. I. Title. II. History of medicine (Enchanted Lion Books)
  R141.D39 2005
  610'.9--dc22   2004061996

Printed and bound in China

Picture Acknowledgements. The author and publisher would like to thank the
following for allowing their pictures to be reproduced in this publication:
AKG 4, 18, 19, 21, 22, 23, 27, 28 Regensburg, Museum der Stadt, 31, 33, 36, 57,
58; Art Archive title page, 5 The Art Archive/Museo Civico Bologna/Dagli Orti, 6 The
Art Archive/Topkapi Museum Istanbul/Dagli Orti, 8 The Art Archive/Real biblioteca
de lo Escorial/Dagli Orti, 9 The Art Archive/Museo del Prado Madrid/Dagli Orti (A),
10 The Art Archive/British Library, 13 The Art Archive/Bodleian Library Oxford, 14
The Art Archive/Bodleian Library Oxford, 15 The Art Archive/Bibliothèque
Universitaire de Mèdecine, Montpellier/Dagli Orti, 17 The Art Archive/ University
Library Prague/Dagli Orti, 20 The Art Archive/University Library Prague/Dagli Orti??,
25 The Art Archive/Biblioteca Nazionale Marciana Venice/ Dagli Orti, 34 The Art
Archive/Bibliothèque Universitaire de Mèdecine, Montpellier/Dagli Orti, 38 The Art
Archive/Biblioteca d'Ajuda Lisbon/ Dagli Orti, 47 The Art Archive/National Library
Cairo/Dagli Orti, 50 The Art Archive/Museum of Islamic Art Cairo/Dagli Orti, 56 The
Art Archive/Victoria and Albert Museum London/Eileen Tweedy, 61?; Bodleian
Library Oxford, 27; Bridgeman/www.bridgeman.co.uk 3, 7 Bibliotheque de la Faculte
de Medecine, Paris, France Archives Charmet, 11 Bibliotheque Municipale, Boulogne-
sur-Mer, France, 12 Bibliotheque de la Faculte de Medecine, Paris, France Archives
Charmet, 16 British Library, London, UK, 30 National Portrait Gallery, London, UK,
43, 45 British Library, London, UK, 59 Biblioteca Civica, Padua, Italy
Bridgeman Art Library/Alinari; British Library 35, 37; Jorvik Museum 40; Philip
Sauvain 39, 42; Topham 24; Trinity College, Cambridge 41; Bayleaf Medieval
Farmstead at the Weald & Downland Open Air Museum, near Chichester, West Sussex
44; Wellcome Library, London 32, 48, 51, 52, 53, 54, 55

Contents

Chapter 1

The fall and rise of medicine

The end of the Roman Empire

The empires of the Greeks and the Romans had lasted for over a thousand years, from 1500 BCE to 400 CE. During this time, doctors advised patients on diet and exercise and made their diagnoses after carefully observing and recording symptoms. They developed a wide range of treatments and a theory that said that people became ill when they had too much or too little of one of the Four Humors (see page 16) in their bodies. They recorded their findings in textbooks. Roman engineers also built sewerage systems, public baths and aqueducts to bring fresh water into towns, all of which helped to safeguard people from disease.

Doctors in the Middle Ages continued to read the books of Hippocrates and Galen. Here a French surgeon teaches his students (on the left) but bows at the same time to the great masters of medicine – Galen, the Arab scholar Avicenna, and Hippocrates (on the right).

Medical developments were possible because the Greek and Roman empires were wealthy, their citizens believed education was important, they had good communications to spread ideas and, above all, they were relatively peaceful. However, by 500 CE the Roman Empire in the west had collapsed. What would this mean for the study of medicine and for the health of the people?

Hippocrates and Galen

The two greatest names in medicine were the Greek, Hippocrates (born c. 460 BCE) and the Roman, Claudius Galen (born 129 CE). We have very little evidence about Hippocrates. In the Middle Ages he was regarded as the "Father of Medicine," the author of many books and as the man who devised the theory of the Four Humors. We now know that these books and the theory were the work of a number of doctors. We know far more about the life of Galen—"The Prince of Physicians"—who built on the work of Hippocrates. Galen's many books became the bedrock of medical training in the Middle Ages.

What were the Middle Ages really like?

The collapse of the Roman Empire in the fifth century was the beginning of the period that we call the Middle Ages. We have many ideas about the Middle Ages, ranging from images of teeming market towns and deadly plague to knightly tournaments and courtly love. We probably also see the Medieval world as more rigid, more difficult, and more threatening than our own. What were the Middle Ages really like and what could people expect from medicine?

Certainly people then had just as much interest in improving medicine, a vital part of everyday life, as people do today. Over the long time span of the Middle Ages, which lasted a thousand years, this concern for improve-ment led to real changes in medicine and in how the body was understood and illnesses were treated—changes which were possible only because many other aspects of daily life underwent profound change as well.

A fifteenth-century painting of the cloth market in Bologna, Italy. It is often said that people in the Middle Ages never left their home villages, but this is not true. Many people travelled a lot in order to trade, go to war or on pilgrimages, or to attend universities. Travel helped to spread ideas, including medical ideas.

War and destruction

The Roman doctor Galen had studied medicine by reading a wide range of textbooks and by visiting the great medical libraries and centers of medical study. The collapse of the western Roman Empire meant that this kind of medical education came to an end.

The Roman Empire had been invaded by peoples the Romans called barbarians. They included the Goths, Franks and Vandals, and the Angles and Saxons. These peoples set up their own small kingdoms. In England, for example, there were at least a dozen kingdoms and it took over 500 years, until about 1000 CE, before one single kingdom of England was securely established.

These small kingdoms were often at war with one another. War destroyed trade, which in turn meant that societies became poorer. This had an impact upon the study of medicine, because wealth had enabled some people to study to become doctors while others used their money to employ doctors. Such luxuries disappeared in the warring kingdoms of western Europe. At the same time, the kings of these warring states were illiterate and so had little interest in the books they found in wealthy houses and monasteries.

In this thirteenth-century illustration from a Turkish manuscript an Arab doctor and his assistant discuss medicine. Arab doctors made important contributions to medical knowledge in the Middle Ages.

Saving medical knowledge

Not all medical books were forgotten or destroyed, however. Some did survive in the libraries of the monasteries throughout Europe. Many others were kept in the great library at Alexandria in Egypt or were translated into Arabic in cities such as Baghdad and Damascus. While Europe was divided by wars, other parts of the world, including Arabia, India and China (see Chapter 6), continued to develop their medical knowledge.

A great deal of everyday medical knowledge also survived amongst ordinary people. Despite the fame of doctors such as Galen, most people in the Roman Empire never saw doctors, who generally treated the rich, soldiers and some townspeople. The women of the family treated the illnesses of ordinary folk in the Roman period, using methods and remedies handed down from mothers to daughters for many generations. This practice continued throughout the Middle Ages, with the same remedies being used in villages throughout Europe, regardless of whether the ruler of the region was a Roman emperor or a medieval king.

A page from an "herbal," a book that showed which plants to use to treat different illnesses. Herbals were detailed books, describing how to make each medicine and how much of each ingredient to use. This example is from a thirteenth-century Islamic herbal.

A cure for paralysis

Many herbal remedies helped the sick, but other treatments would have been less helpful! They were a mixture of religion, magic and folklore, such as this cure from *Bald's Leechbook*, a book of Anglo-Saxon remedies written in about 900 CE:

...scarify [scratch] the neck after the setting of the sun and silently pour the blood into running water. After that, spit three times, then say: Have thou this unheal and depart with it.

Religion and medicine

Religion, including both Christianity and Islam, played a central part in medicine in the Middle Ages. Monasteries did not just preserve medical books from destruction but used their treatments and medicines in the monastic infirmaries. One of the rules of the Benedictine monks stated: "the care of the sick is to be placed above and before every other duty." Monks were treated in the monastic infirmary, while local people could be treated and given remedies by the infirmerer who was in charge of the infirmary.

Practical treatments went hand in hand with the belief that prayer could cure the sick. The Bible told how Jesus Christ had healed the sick and the Christian Church promised that the saints would answer prayers. Each part of the body and each ailment had its own saint. For example, sufferers from backache prayed to Saint Lawrence. Saint Sebastian was expected to keep

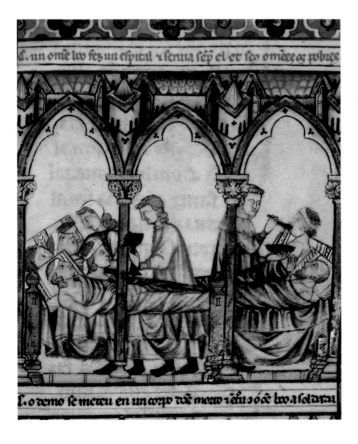

Monastic infirmaries throughout Europe provided good care for sick monks and the employees of the monastery. This care usually involved patients being kept warm and clean and being fed, simple treatments that often did people a great deal of good.

plague at bay. Saint Apollonia was the patron saint of toothache because all her teeth had been broken with pincers while she was being persecuted for her religion. Women in childbirth prayed to Saint Margaret of Antioch. It was said that a dragon had swallowed Saint Margaret whole but, when inside the dragon's stomach, she made the sign of the cross, which turned into a real cross and grew until the dragon burst open and Saint Margaret could step out!

The rise of universities

The climate in Europe between the years 1000 and 1300 was ideal for agriculture, with high average temperatures and good but not over heavy rainfall. Many harvests were excellent and so landowners grew rich. The wealthiest landowners of all were the rulers of the Christian Church, the bishops and abbots. They spent their profits on building grand cathedrals and on education, founding universities such as Paris in 1110, Bologna in 1158, Oxford in 1167, Cambridge in 1209 and Padua in 1222. These universities played a major part in the development of the study of medicine, along with the medical school at Salerno in Italy, which was founded in about 1100.

A fifteenth-century painting of the patron saints of medicine, Saint Cosmas and Saint Damian, performing their miraculous transplant (see panel). Saint Cosmas became the patron saint of physicians and Saint Damian the patron saint of surgeons.

The patron saints of medicine

The Greeks and Romans had prayed to the gods Asclepius and Salus for help when they were ill. In the Middle Ages, Damian and Cosmas became the patron saints of medicine. They were brothers from Cilicia (in present-day southern Turkey) who were famous for healing the sick. It was believed that they had performed a miracle by transplanting the leg of a black man on to a white man, whose leg had been amputated because of gangrene. The procedure didn't work, but people believed a miracle had taken place. They became saints after they were murdered for their Christian beliefs.

Chapter 2

Who could you turn to if you were ill?

Women and medicine

Women treated the vast majority of illnesses and were expected to have a wide range of remedies at their fingertips. If the problem did not get better, then the local wise-woman was called in. A wise-woman was the name given to a local woman regarded by others as having special skills and knowledge of medicine.

Women were able to qualify as surgeons by working as apprentices to qualified surgeons. Family links played an important part in giving women this opportunity. Records show that a woman named Katherine was a surgeon in London around 1250, and that her father and brothers were all surgeons. By the 1380s master-surgeons were required to take an oath, which required them to keep "faithful oversight of all others, both men and women, occupied in the art of surgery."

Everyday healthcare, shown in a fifteenth-century illustration from a Bible. The woman by the fire is preparing a herbal remedy and checking the recipe in her commonplace book of useful information.

However, women could not become physicians – university-trained doctors who had a much higher status than surgeons. The Church did not allow women to attend universities, and even women from wealthy families received very little education. This did not stop some determined women from practising medicine. Hildegard of Bingen in Germany (1098–1179) was a nun who practised medicine and wrote medical textbooks about the use of "simples," which were herbs, vegetables and animal parts.

No women allowed!

Men objected to women taking their work. In the 1420s, leading doctors in England sent a petition to parliament asking for a ban on women working as doctors. They shared the views of John of Mirfield, a fourteenth-century doctor, who wrote:

"Worthless and presumptuous women take over this profession. They possess neither natural ability nor professional knowledge. They make the greatest possible mistakes thanks to their stupidity and very often kill the patients. They work without wisdom and without any foundation of knowledge."

This fifteenth-century French illustration shows midwives at the birth of a prince. In some towns midwives had to be apprenticed to doctors and gain licenses. They were then paid for their expertise.

Women on trial

In 1322 five women were put on trial in Paris for practising medicine without a licence. Jacqueline Felicie de Almania was charged with visiting the sick and "feeling their pulses, examining their urine and touching their limbs." Eight of her patients testified on her behalf, saying that she had cured them when male doctors had failed, but the judge found all the women guilty, saying: "It is certain that a man qualified in medicine could cure the sick better than any woman." All the women were excommunicated, a terrible punishment meaning they were not allowed to attend any church services and would be certain to go to Hell when they died.

Ego determinatis vobis in isto quinto libro utilitates antidotorum medicinaliū modum conficien di ea

A teacher at the University of Paris, giving a lecture and reading aloud from a book by Ibn Sina, the great Arab medical scholar (known as "Avicenna" in Europe). The student on the right may be following the reading in his own book while an assistant mixes medicines.

The growth of university training

Wealthy people from the eleventh century onwards could pay to see a university-trained physician if they became ill. The first university medical school was founded at Salerno, Italy in about 1100. Salerno was well placed geographically to have contact with both the Greek-speaking world of the Mediterranean and the Arabic-speaking world, where standards of medicine were high.

By the twelfth century there were medical schools at universities throughout Europe, yet they did not all have large numbers of students. It took seven years of study to qualify as a physician, which must have put off many who were not from wealthy families. At Bologna in Italy, one of the most advanced medical schools, an average of only four doctors qualified each year in the early fifteenth century.

Training to be a physician

Medical students attended lectures and read a set list of books. Galen's writings were at the heart of this list, along with the works of Hippocrates, other Greek and Roman writers and translations of Arab scholars such as Ibn Sina and al-Razi (also known as "Rhazes" in the west). Students were expected to memorize what these great doctors had written. They were not expected to challenge their ideas. In 1278 the English scientist Roger Bacon suggested that doctors should do their own research instead of just reading Galen; church leaders reacted by throwing him into prison. It was rare for students to do any practical work, but at both Paris and Bologna students had to work with a qualified physician before they could qualify themselves.

Another crucial part of medical education was astrology. Students learned how each part of the body was affected by the movements of the planets and stars. A doctor needed to know the position of the planets before making a diagnosis and deciding on a treatment.

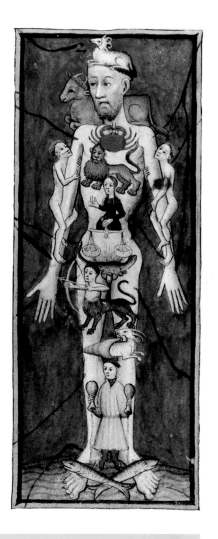

The Zodiac Man was one of the three most common illustrations in medieval medical books, and it showed the doctor when to avoid treating each part of the body. When the moon was in Pisces, for example, doctors should not treat the feet. This Zodiac Man is from an English book produced *c.* 1424.

How a doctor should behave

Codes of behavior were laid down for doctors by writers such as the French surgeon Guy de Chauliac (see page 15):

A doctor should be willing to learn, be sober and modest, charming, hard-working and intelligent. He should take care of the rich and poor, for medicine is needed by all classes of people. If payment is offered, he should accept rather than refuse it. But if it is not offered, it should not be demanded. Whatever is heard in the course of treatment should be kept secret.

To dissect or not to dissect?

It seems strange today that the training of doctors in the Middle Ages was not dominated by practical learning through dissection and working with live patients. Instead, students learned about anatomy (the structure of the body) and physiology (the workings of the body) through reading, particularly books by Galen. This was partly because the Christian Church, which controlled the universities, believed that ancient writings should be believed and not questioned. They said that Galen's theories were correct and so there was little point in dissecting bodies because nothing new would be learned.

A priest catches a man illegally dissecting a body. This illustration is from an English manuscript produced c. 1292.

One reason why Galen was so influential was because he believed that each part of the body had a definite purpose. His view was in line with the Christian belief that God had created human beings and therefore the human body must be a perfect creation. Christian leaders went so far as to say that anyone who questioned Galen was also questioning God, which was forbidden.

The beginning of new ideas

Nevertheless, ideas did begin to change in the fourteenth century as university physicians wanted to find out more about anatomy and the Church's power to stop them declined. Students at Bologna University were the first to be required to attend the dissection of a corpse as part of their studies. In fact, human dissections became an important, if small, part of medical education in Italy and Spain. It wasn't until the sixteenth century, however, that universities in England and Germany followed this approach.

Students did not dissect the bodies themselves, but rather watched from the tiered seats of anatomy theaters. The professor, a qualified physician, would read from Galen's works while the surgeon cut into the body of a newly-dead criminal. Sometimes the "ostensor" pointed out the parts of the body. These dissections were dramatic performances with students cramming into the theaters, craning their necks to get a better view. In all likelihood the dissections added little to the students' knowledge, but it was the beginning of an important development in medical education.

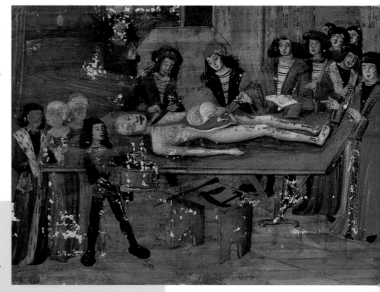

A public dissection at the University of Montpellier in France. The students standing in the doorway would not have been able to see or learn much from where they were. This illustration is from *De Chirurgia* (On Surgery) by Guy de Chauliac (see panel).

Books or dissection?

Guy de Chauliac was a French surgeon who lived *c.* 1300–1380. He wrote well-known medical books and was prepared to challenge old ideas. In one book he wrote:

Knowledge of anatomy is gained in two ways. One is by books. This is useful but it is not enough to discover all that can be learned by observation. The second way is by dissecting dead bodies, namely of those who have been recently beheaded or hanged. By this we learn the anatomy of the internal organs, the muscles, skin, veins and sinews.

Explanations for illness

There were many different explanations for illness.
Throughout the Middle Ages, the most common belief
was that God and the Devil caused sickness. People
believed that plagues such as the Black Death (see page
24) were sent by God to punish people for their sins.
The Devil was often blamed for more everyday
ailments, such as headaches. The Anglo-Saxons
believed that elves and spirits were the Devil's helpers,
shooting invisible arrows, known as "elf-shot," which
caused these ailments. Another common everyday belief
was that worms were the cause of illness. This idea is
not as strange as it sounds. We know from
archaeological discoveries that many people
suffered from worms in their stomachs and that
they would have seen the worms in
their faeces.

Four Humors

Doctors, especially those trained in universities
in the later Middle Ages, continued to believe in
the theory of the Four Humors. It stated that
illnesses were caused when the Four Humors or
liquids in the body (blood, phlegm, black bile
and yellow bile) fell out of balance. Therefore
doctors treating the sick tried to make them well

**A doctor and his assistants
diagnose the patient's illness
by examining his urine.**

Fear doctors!

Many Romans had been suspicious of doctors and this attitude continued in the Middle
Ages. The fourteenth-century Italian author Plutarch copied the words of the Roman
writer Pliny when he wrote to Pope Clement VI:

*I know that your bedside is besieged by doctors and naturally this fills me with
fear. They learn their art at our expense and even our death brings them
experience. Oh, Most Gentle Father, look upon their band as an army of enemies.*

In England, John of Salisbury warned of doctors, because, he said, their motto was:

Take your fee while the patient is sick as he cannot pay when he is dead.

by restoring the balance of the humors, usually by reducing the quantity of the humor that they believed was dominant. This idea had been developed by Hippocrates and Galen and so became a standard part of university training as their books were so widely read.

Diagnosing the illness

The most important piece of equipment used by a physician to diagnose an illness was a urine chart. The physician checked the color of the patient's urine against a chart. He also checked its smell and even taste. Wealthy patients regularly sent their urine to be checked by their physician to make sure that they were not becoming ill. This method of diagnosis fitted in with the theory of the Four Humors. For example, physicians believed that if the urine was too white, it was a sign of too much phlegm in the body. Using this information, the physician then worked out how to treat his patient.

A urine chart was one of the physician's essential tools. The physician matched the patient's urine against the colors, smell and density shown on the chart.

Going to the hospital

Many hospitals were founded in the later Middle Ages because looking after the sick was an important part of the work of the Christian Church. European cities such as Paris and Florence had large civic hospitals and Florence (a city of 30,000 people) had another 30 smaller hospitals too. St Bartholomew's Hospital in London was founded in 1123; by 1400 there were over 500 hospitals in England. However, very few were big. While St. Leonard's in York had over 200 beds, most had only five or six.

Many hospitals were built for people suffering from leprosy, a disfiguring skin disease. By 1225 there were 19,000 leprosy hospitals in Europe. Occasionally, hospitals were set up to care for other particular kinds of cases. In London, Richard Whittington, three times Lord Mayor, paid for the building of an eight-bed ward for unmarried pregnant women. In Chester there was a hospital for the care of "poor and silly persons."

The key difference between hospitals then and now is that then hospitals were not places to go to if you

On the right you can see a patient being brought into the Hotel Dieu, a hospital in Paris, while a new nun arrives on the left. Much of a nun's day would be spent caring for the sick. This illustration and the one opposite are from a book showing daily life in the Hotel Dieu, which was written c. 1483.

The rules of a hospital

From the rules of the hospital of St John, Bridgwater in the south of England, 1219:

No lepers, lunatics or persons having the falling sickness or other contagious disease, and no pregnant women, or sucking infants and no intolerable persons, even though they be poor and infirm, are to be admitted. If any such be admitted by mistake they are to be expelled as soon as possible. And when the other poor and infirm persons have recovered they are to be let out without delay.

Here nuns are being trained in a ward in the hospital of the Hotel Dieu in Paris. The nuns kept the patients warm, clean and well-fed.

were sick! The great majority cared for the old and infirm. They were more like elderly homes than modern-day hospitals. When people came to the door of a hospital they were carefully checked over to make sure that they were respectable and were not carrying any infectious disease. If they were, they were sent away, for fear of infecting everyone in the hospital.

Hospitals provided food, rest, perhaps some herbal remedies and prayer. At the end of the ward, there was an altar where the priests said mass every day. The patients joined in the prayers from their beds. The nuns provided nursing care, making sure that the patients were well fed, warm and rested. The nuns also had a good knowledge of herbal remedies, which they often drew from the books in their library.

Chapter 3

How did they treat the sick in the Middle Ages?

Qualified physicians found work treating wealthy patients—merchants, noblemen and women, and kings. Their first duty was to give advice on how to stay healthy by suggesting changes to diet and plenty of exercise. This approach was very similar to that of Greek and Roman doctors. Physicians employed by King Edward III of England during his reign in the 1300s had their duties laid down. They included:

"...talk with the steward and the master cook to devise what meats and drinks are best for the king ... also spy if anyone in the court be infected with leprosy or pestilence and to warn the king to keep him out of the court until he be well."

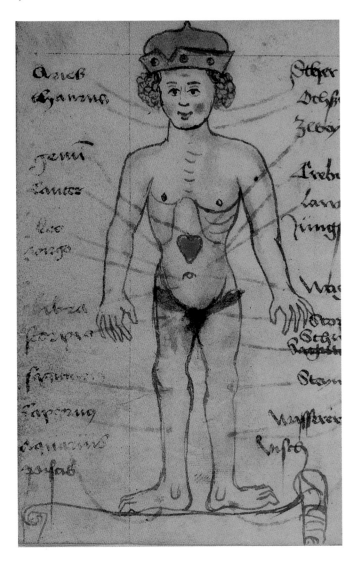

This drawing of the human body shows how a patient can be safely bled according to the movements of the stars and the planets. The arrows point to the veins that were the main bleeding points. This type of chart, along with urine and zodiac charts, were the three most common illustrations in medical books.

Bleeding

Often physicians tried to restore the proper balance of the patient's humours by purging or bleeding the patient, which meant taking blood from the patient's body by opening a vein. According to medical books, bleeding:

"...clears the mind, strengthens the memory, cleanses the guts, sharpens the hearing, curbs tears, promotes digestion, produces a musical voice, dispels sleepiness, drives away anxiety, feeds the blood and rids it of poisonous matter and gives long life, cures pains, fevers and various sicknesses and makes urine clear and clean."

Not surprisingly, bleeding was carried out frequently. Records from monasteries show that monks could be bled between seven and twelve times a year to prevent illness. On occasion this was carried out until the monk was on the point of unconsciousness, which means he must have lost one or two quarts of blood!

Techniques used for bleeding included warming a bleeding cup, placing it over a small cut and letting the warmth draw blood out of the cut. Alternatively, physicians used leeches to sink their jaws into the patient and draw off blood.

An apprehensive patient looks away as blood is being taken from her arm. This illustration comes from a fifteenth-century manuscript on the plague.

The wonder of leeches

Using leeches sounds barbaric, but they are used today for good scientific reasons. Scientists discovered that the saliva of leeches stops blood clotting. They can draw off this saliva to treat people who develop blood clots in the brain – the saliva also breaks down the clot. Doctors also use leeches when patients have had fingers or ears sewn back on after accidents. Sometimes too much blood can build up at the site of a wound, when blood arrives through the arteries at a faster rate than the veins can take it away. This stops the veins from healing, but if leeches are applied to the spot, they suck up the excess blood and so help the veins heal!

Did herbal remedies work?

The most common remedies were based on minerals, animal parts and particularly plants or herbs. Physicians were expected to have detailed knowledge of such remedies, and so too was every wife and mother. Remedies were collected in herbals, which detailed the exact quantities of all the ingredients required, gave instructions for mixing the potion, and even referred to the medical problem itself. For example, a page recommending the use of crowsfoot for dog bites was illustrated with a scene showing a dog or wolf biting a hunter's leg! Another page showed a fox, recommending that its liver and lungs, chopped up and taken in wine, were good for asthma!

Many of the ingredients in these remedies would in fact have been helpful to sufferers. Honey was a common ingredient and had been used to kill infections in ancient Egypt from approximately 2000 BCE. Another ingredient was plantain, a plant that features in *Bald's Leechbook* in 48 different remedies, largely for cuts, wounds, dog bites and boils. Modern scientific analysis of these remedies has shown that 25 of the 48 remedies would have been helpful, because plantain acts like a modern antibiotic in fighting infection.

This fifteenth-century illustration shows women at work in their garden. Most monasteries, convents and manor houses had herb gardens for growing plants that could be used in medicine. Saying prayers while collecting the herbs was believed to make the remedy more effective.

How to cure a stye on the eye

This cure comes from *Bald's Leechbook*, written in the tenth century:

Take equal amounts of onion and garlic and pound them well together. Take equal amounts of wine and bull's gall and mix them with the onion and garlic. Put the mixture in a brass bowl and let it stand for nine nights, then strain it through a cloth. Then, about night-time, apply it to the eye with a feather.

Did it work? Yes, it probably did. The onion, garlic and bull's gall all attack bacteria that cause styes. The wine contains acetic acid; this reacts with the copper in the brass bowl to form copper salts, which also kill bacteria.

The plants that were used in herbal remedies were deliberately cultivated so that they would be available when needed. In the late fourteenth century, Hugh Daniel, a churchman, grew over 250 different herbs in his "physic garden." Many remedies involved using a large number of plants and it was assumed that a housewife would have these in her garden or be able to collect them from nearby hedgerows or fields. A common remedy to ease the pain of bruises and wounds included a mixture of comfrey, knapweed, marigold, yarrow, wood avens, root of wallwort, clover, wild sage, dock, madder and several other plants.

An apothecary's shop, shown in a fourteenth-century Italian manuscript. This was where townspeople could buy the ingredients for herbal remedies.

The arrival of the Black Death

How well did doctors and other healers cope when they were faced by an epidemic of disease? In 1348 they faced one of the most severe outbreaks of disease in history—bubonic plague—known as the "Black Death." The epidemic began in China, spread to India and across Europe. It was carried on trading ships by fleas, which nestled in the coats of black rats. The fleas passed on the disease when they bit people. The victims suddenly felt shivery and tired and then discovered painful swellings called "buboes" in their armpits and groins. Blisters appeared all over their bodies, followed by high fever, severe headaches, unconsciousness and finally death.

In 1348 the pestilence, as it was called at the time, arrived in England and spread rapidly. According to one chronicler, the Black Death left "not a town, a village

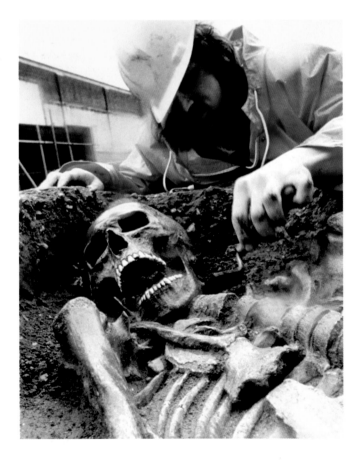

A victim of the Black Death recently excavated from the grounds of Hereford Cathedral in England. The death rate was so high that in many places new burial grounds were needed to cope with the number of bodies.

or even, except rarely a house, without killing most or all of the people there. As a result there was such a shortage of people that there were hardly enough living to bury the dead." At least 40 per cent of the population died, and towns and ports were even harder hit. Only remote villages and farms high up on the hills were likely to be safe. There

were more major outbreaks throughout Europe during the rest of the fourteenth century, (England was hit in 1361, 1369, 1374 and again in 1390), and minor epidemics sprang up in individual towns.

As their friends died around them, people felt despair and hopelessness. An Irish monk, Brother John Clynn, wrote down an account of the plague and then concluded:

"I, waiting among the dead for death to come, leave parchment for continuing the work, in case anyone should still be alive in the future and any son of Adam can escape this pestilence and continue my work."

This fourteenth-century illustration creates a vivid sense of chaos and confusion which arose from so many people dying from the Black Death in such a short space of time. More heart-wrenching evidence can be seen on the church wall in Ashwell in Hertfordshire, England, where these words were scratched: "1349 the pestilence 1350 pitiless, wild, violent, the dregs of the people live to tell the tale."

The impact of the Black Death

How did it feel to have lived through the Black Death? The Italian writer Petrarch wrote this to a friend in 1350:

Where are our dear friends now? Where are the beloved faces? Where are the affectionate words, the relaxed and enjoyable conversations? What lightning bolt devoured them? What earthquake topped them? There was a crowd of us, now we are almost alone. We should make new friends, but how, when the human race is almost wiped out; and why, when it looks to me as if the end of the world is at hand?

One physician takes the victim's pulse while the other examines his urine, but even these wealthy and successful physicians cannot stop death from taking their patient. This warning comes from a fifteenth-century French manuscript.

What did they think caused the Black Death?

In September 1348, as the Black Death rampaged across England, the Prior of Christchurch Abbey, Canterbury wrote:

"Terrible is God towards the sons of men ...He often allows plagues, miserable famines, conflicts, wars and other suffering to arise, and uses them to terrify and torment men and so drive out their sins. Thus the realm of England, because of the increasing pride and numberless sins of the people is struck by the pestilence."

The most common explanation for the pestilence, among ordinary people as well as churchmen, was that God was punishing the people for their sins. Physicians, of course, said that the answer could be found in the books of Galen. One physician, John of Burgundy, pointed out:

"As Galen says in his book on fevers, the body does not become sick unless it already contains evil humors. The pestilential air does no harm to cleansed bodies from which evil humors have been purged."

Desperate explanations

As millions died, a wide range of other explanations were put forward. An English monk blamed the outrageous fashions that people had been wearing in recent years. Another writer said that so many had died because earthquakes had infected the air. Inevitably, minority groups were blamed. Jews were said to have poisoned water supplies. In some towns Jews were burned as people desperately looked for someone to blame for the disaster.

However, not all explanations were so wide of the mark. Some people did make a correct connection between the disease and the dirt the rats fed on. The work of John Jacobus, a doctor at the famous medical school at Montpellier in France, led to the suggestion that:

"Sometimes the pestilence comes from a privy toilet next to a chamber or some other thing that corrupts the air. Sometimes it comes from dead flesh or from standing water in ditches."

Guy de Chauliac, the most celebrated surgeon of the 14th century, even while striving to eliminate astrology from surgery, noted that "...the close position of Saturn, Jupiter and Mars ... is always a sign of wonderful, terrible or violent things to come." This fifteenth-century English illustration reveals how people believed the planets affected humans. Saturn at the top is eating his children, while Jupiter at the bottom throws thunderbolts.

Obey your parents!

In 1361 there was another outbreak of plague in England that killed many children. They had not been born when the Black Death first struck in 1348 and so had not been alive to build up natural immunity when the disease recurred. This led an anonymous churchman to suggest:

If your father and mother are in need because of their age or misfortune, children are bound to help them, both with your body and your possessions. If they are dead you are bound to pray night and day to God to deliver them from pain. God has sent the pestilence to slay the children because they have been dishonoring and despising their fathers and mothers.

How did they try to stop the Black Death?

As they did not understand the real cause of the plague, doctors could do nothing to help the victims. Even the French doctor Guy de Chauliac admitted: "Doctors were useless and indeed shameful especially as they dared not visit the sick for fear of becoming infected. When they did visit them, there was little they could do." Guy himself recommended bleeding and purges to empty the bowels. This would simply have weakened sufferers even further.

The only practical way of stopping the spread of the disease was to isolate newcomers. In Italy, city states, such as Venice, stopped travellers entering the city. At Ragusa (present-day Dubrovnik) newcomers had to spend 30 days in a place distant from the town to see if they developed the disease. This was later extended to 40 days, or *quarantenaria* in Italian, from which the word "quarantine" comes.

Plague sufferers in the late Middle Ages prayed to St Roch, the patron saint of plague victims. He caught the plague in Rome in the fourteenth century, survived and apparently miraculously cured other sufferers. This sixteenth-century painting shows him, on the left, suffering from the plague outside a plague hospital. On the right, he is curing plague victims .

Prayers and candles

Most people turned to prayer because they believed that the pestilence was a punishment from God. Kings and bishops ordered priests to lead processions in which people prayed for forgiveness and asked God to put an end to the disease. Some people made candles their own height and lit them in church as offerings to God.

In Barcelona, the citizens made a candle over four miles long, which they hoped would encircle and protect the city.

Believers expected God to listen. After all, the Bible contained 35 examples of Jesus healing the sick and the saints continued his work. At Winchester, local people believed in God's healing powers because they could see, at the cathedral, evidence of God's willingness to answer the prayers of the sick. The cathedral was "hung all round with crutches and with the stools of cripples who had been healed" after visiting the tomb of Saint Swithun – a testament to the belief in the power of prayer.

This mid-fourteenth century illustration shows flagellants in the Netherlands. Flagellants walked through towns as the plague spread, whipping themselves to show God that they had repented their sins and asking Him to be merciful.

How to avoid the plague

This advice comes from John of Burgundy, the author of one of the first books about the plague, written in 1365:

Avoid too much eating and drinking and avoid baths which open the pores, for the pores are doorways through which poisonous air can enter the body. In cold or rainy weather, light fires in your room. In foggy or windy weather, inhale perfumes every morning before leaving home. If the plague arrives during hot weather, eat cold things rather than hot and drink more than you eat. Be sparing with hot substances such as pepper, garlic, onions and everything else that generates excessive heat and instead use cucumbers, fennel and spinach.

Chapter 4

How effective was medieval surgery?

Saving Prince Henry's life

Henry V, one of the greatest kings of England, is best remembered for leading his army to a great victory over the French at Agincourt in 1415. The main reason for the English victory at Agincourt was the longbow. Ironically, Henry himself had nearly been killed by an arrow from a longbow twelve years earlier, at the battle of Shrewsbury, and his life had been saved by the skills of an army surgeon.

The battle of Shrewsbury was fought during a rebellion by a group of noblemen against Henry's father, King Henry IV. As the battle began, the rebel archers released a storm of arrows into the royal army. These arrows had the power to penetrate plate armor and then kill a man. One arrow, glancing off the curve of a helmet, thudded into the left cheek of young Prince Henry. The prince fell to the ground, but much of the force of the arrow had been spent on the helmet and this saved his life. The arrowhead, however, had still penetrated to the back of his skull.

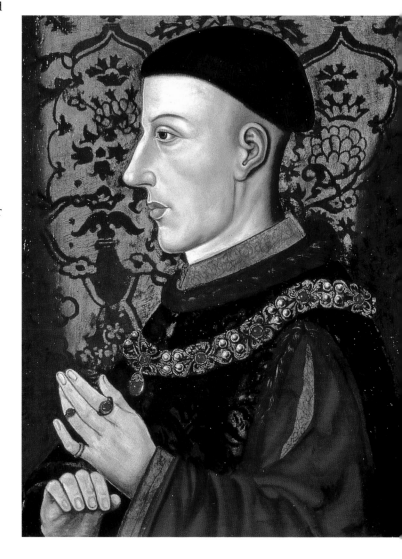

The young Prince who underwent surgery after a battle lived to become Henry V, King of England from 1413–1422.

The shaft of the arrow was cut off and the sixteen-year-old prince fought on. The battle ended in victory for the prince. Afterwards his surgeon, John Bradmore, faced an almost impossible task. He could not see exactly where the arrowhead was, but it had to be removed without fragmenting and leaving pieces in the wound. Bradmore did not understand the science of infection but knew from experience that the wound could easily become infected and kill the heir to the throne.

First Bradmore designed a metal forcep to pass through the cheek wound, take hold of the arrowhead and then pull it out. While a blacksmith worked to make the new instrument, Blackmore kept the wound open by pushing wooden probes through it, each time using a wider probe to enlarge the hole. Each probe was wrapped in clean linen, smeared with honey, which was good for keeping wounds free of infection.

Eventually Bradmore was able to push the new forcep through the wound, locate the arrowhead and remove it. For the next three weeks, he dressed the wound with barley and honey. It healed free from any infection. Bradmore's use of a traditional remedy, honey, and his invention of a new instrument had saved the Prince's life.

A fifteenth-century illustration of medical care on a military campaign. Henry V, not surprisingly after his experience at Shrewsbury, took twelve surgeons to care for his army when he invaded France in 1415.

The madness of King Henry VI

Henry VI, King of England from 1422–1461 and 1470–71, suffered a period of mental illness in 1453–54 when he fell into a stupor, unable to speak, recognize anyone or make decisions. When he fell ill, his doctors used a range of treatments to help the king recover. Their main treatment was to restore the proper balance of the humors in the king's body by bathing, purging or bleeding him. His diet was carefully regulated to reduce the impact of the cold, wet humors associated with being in a stupor. So he was fed plenty of hot dishes, such as chicken broth. Henry recovered after eighteen months but soon afterwards fell ill again and continued to suffer from mental illness until he was murdered by his successor, Edward IV.

Developments in surgery

John Bradmore's skills help to explain why there were new discoveries and developments in surgery during the Middle Ages. Many surgeons gained valuable experience on the battlefield, where they came across problems forcing them to devise new methods or try new techniques. Away from the battlefield, surgeons trained as apprentices to qualified surgeons. Guilds of Master-Surgeons controlled entrance to the profession; they required new members to gain licenses by passing tests. Surgeons therefore learned their skills through practice, unlike the university-trained physicians who gained their knowledge from the books of Galen and other ancient writers.

Despite their practical training, surgeons in England were seen as inferior to physicians, because they had not been to university. In France and Italy, however, surgeons taught at universities, demonstrating that they could be as well educated as physicians. In around 1180, Roger of Salerno (also known as Roger Frugardi) was the author of the first textbook on surgery to be written in western Europe. His book was used throughout Europe to train surgeons.

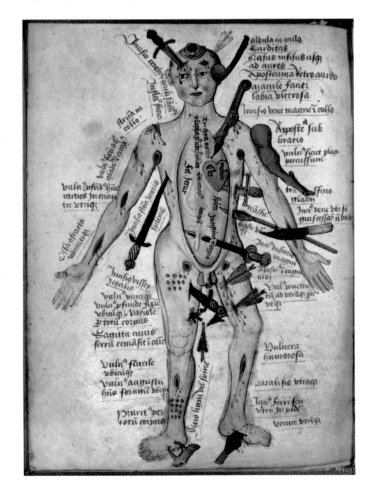

A "wound man" was a common medical illustration; it showed the wounds that surgeons could treat successfully and others they could find treatments for in the medical textbooks.

Guy de Chauliac

The greatest surgeon of the later Middle Ages was a Frenchman called Guy de Chauliac (1298–1368). De Chauliac was educated at the universities of Bologna and Montpellier and he dedicated himself to improving the quality of surgery and advancing it as equal to the general medical practice of the physician. His great work was the seven-volume *Chirurgia Magna (Great Surgery)*, which was a standard surgical text for three centuries. It is filled with references to the works of great doctors, with 890 quotations from Galen, 661 from the Arab scholar Ibn Sina, 120 from Hippocrates, and many more. The embodiment of erudition, de Chauliac also demonstrated the practical qualities of being a surgeon. He devised a bedframe that made it easier for patients to turn. He recommended new ways to splint a fracture, and he used weights to stretch a broken limb and help it heal more cleanly.

An illustration from Roger of Salerno's textbook on surgery, showing a surgeon examining his patients.

A surgeon must be ...

In the fourteenth century Guy de Chauliac listed these essential qualities for a surgeon:

The surgeon needs to have four qualities: first, he should be learned. He should know not only the principles of surgery but also those of medicine in theory and in practice. Second, he should be expert at the practice of surgery; third, he must be ingenious and fourth, he should be able to adapt himself.

A common method of closing wounds was to seal them with a burning iron. This was known as cauterizing a wound. Here a surgeon cauterizes an arm wound, much to the patient's discomfort.

Galen could be wrong!

The greatest surgical debate in the Middle Ages was about the unpleasant topic of pus! Since the time of the Greeks, doctors had said that wounds were more likely to heal if certain kinds of pus (known as "laudable" or "praiseworthy" pus) developed. They believed the pus carried away poisoned blood that caused infection. Doctors therefore covered wounds in ointments and bandages designed to make pus develop.

Then came a father and son who dared to say that this idea was wrong! Hugh of Lucca became surgeon to the city of Bologna in Italy in 1214. He accompanied the city's soldiers on a Crusade and taught medicine at the city's university. Hugh's son, Theodoric (1205–1296), also became a surgeon and writer. In his textbook, Theodoric dared to say:

"It is not necessary that pus should be formed in wounds. There can be no greater mistake than this! Such a procedure is quite against nature, prolongs illness, prevents healing and hinders the closing up of wounds. My father used to heal almost every kind of wound with wine alone, and he produced the most beautiful healing without any ointments."

Thinking for themselves

Hugh's methods would have been effective. Wine, like honey, attacks infections. However, most surgeons could not bring themselves to accept this new idea and carried on with the old methods. One man who agreed with Hugh was Henri de Mondeville (*c.*1260–*c.*1320), a military surgeon who studied surgery at Bologna with Theodoric and became a teacher at Paris. He taught his students to bathe and cleanse wounds, then close them up quickly without trying to form pus.

The work of Hugh and Theodoric and Henri de Mondeville shows that some doctors were prepared to think for themselves and even challenge the words of Galen and the other ancient writers. Even though few others agreed with them, this was the beginning of important changes in the study of medicine.

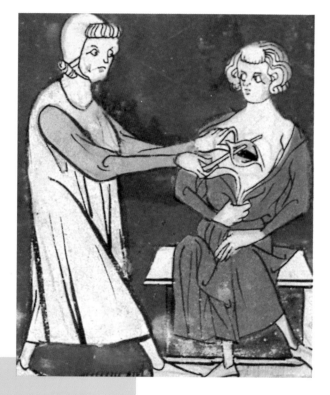

A fourteenth-century illustration showing a wound being sewn up. The artist has enlarged the cut and the needle so that readers can see them more easily.

A challenge to Galen

Henri de Mondeville wrote a surgical textbook in which he dared to suggest that the works of Galen did not contain everything there was to be known about medicine. Two of his famous statements were: "We now know things which were unknown in Galen's time and it is our duty to clarify them in our writings," and "God surely didn't use up all his genius on Galen", suggesting that surgeons of his own time could make new and important discoveries. Ironically, Henri was fiercely outspoken and impatient with less clever colleagues, just like Galen himself!

Everyday surgery

While a handful of university surgeons dared to challenge ancient ideas, most surgeons carried out a range of simple operations. They were very similar to the kinds of operations carried out in the Greek and Roman periods. Surgeons removed small tumors on the surface of the skin, sewed up or cauterized large cuts, and dealt with dislocations or broken limbs. The most skilful used extremely fine needles to remove cataracts from eyes, thereby restoring or improving people's sight. Some surgeons were able to remove stones that had grown and lodged, extremely painfully, in the bladder. Trepanning (the process of cutting a hole in the skull) continued to be successfully carried out, just as it had

A surgeon removes a cataract from his patient's eye. The patient is holding a jar of ointment ready to be applied to the eye. The most common providers of surgery were known as barber-surgeons because they combined shaving and hair-cutting with bleeding, tooth-pulling and other basic surgical tasks. Their skills varied considerably, but some joined recognized "guilds" and served apprenticeships.

been since prehistoric times. This operation repaired head wounds and also relieved severe headaches and pressure on the brain.

The problem of pain

Although even the more intricate standard operations had a good chance of being successful because the surgeons had developed their skills through experience, nevertheless, complex surgery inside the body still could not be performed. To do this they would have needed more detailed knowledge of anatomy. They also needed effective ways of anesthetizing patients for longer than a few moments. Medieval surgeons did not ignore pain. They did the best they could by using anaesthetic sponges soaked in mandrake, opium or hemlock, which did, at least, make patients drowsy. But there was always the danger of using too much of a drug, such as opium, and putting the patient to sleep permanently.

A barber-surgeon or tooth-puller removes a tooth, from an illustration *c.* 1360. You can see why many patients had to be held down when having a tooth taken out!

A medieval anaesthetic

A fourteenth-century medical book recommended this mixture as an anaesthetic:

To make a drink that men call dwale, to make a man sleep during an operation. Take the gall of a boar, three spoonfuls of the juice of hemlock and three spoonfuls of wild briony, lettuce, opium poppy, henbane and vinegar. Mix them well together and then let the man sit by a good fire and make him drink of the potion until he falls asleep. Then he may safely be operated upon.

Another problem that surgeons could not tackle was severe blood loss. No one understood that people had different blood groups or how to undertake a blood transfusion. These surgical problems of pain and blood loss, together with the immense danger of infection developing inside the body, would not be solved until the middle of the nineteenth century.

Chapter 5

Were medieval towns really so unhealthy?

One day in 1326 a man walking down Cheap Street in London threw some rubbish into the lane between two shops. That doesn't sound like an unusual event, since we easily might think of the streets in medieval towns as being fairly dirty places. But what happened next might make us think again. The apprentices from the shops who had seen the man throwing away his eel skins rushed outside and beat him up, angry that he had left litter near their shops.

We know about this story because the man died from his injuries and the apprentices were taken to court. The story tells us that life could be very violent in a large city in the Middle Ages, but it also suggests a real concern with hygiene, even if medieval cities were dirtier and more chaotic than not. We can investigate this concern with cleanliness by looking at the changes in York, which was an important city from the Roman period right through to the end of the Middle Ages.

Bathing in a medieval tub, shown in a manuscript illustration of 1356 entitled *Treatise on Medicine*. **The rich were able to wash and bath regularly and believed cleanliness helped to keep them healthy.**

By order of the King!

A Royal Order by Edward III in 1357 stated:

Order – to cause the bank of the River Thames and the streets and lanes of the city to be cleansed of dung, dungheaps and other filth and to keep them clean. In the time of the King's ancestors the streets used to be cleansed of refuse and filth but now, in crossing the River Thames, the King has observed filth and other refuse accumulated on the bank. Noisome smells arise therefrom, whereby great danger may arise to men dwelling in the city.

Roman York

Roman York sounds as if it was a very healthy place. Aqueducts brought in fresh water and lead pipes took it to individual buildings. Sewers took away waste and there were baths where the public could wash and exercise. These facilities did help the citizens of York stay healthy, but it wasn't quite as wonderful as it sounds. The sewers were too large and there wasn't enough fast-running water to flush them out properly. This meant that sewage simply sat in the bottom of the pipes and this led to disease spreading. The sewers also emptied into the local river, where people washed their clothes and collected drinking water. Again this led to the spread of disease.

This late medieval illustration from Germany shows people emptying household waste of all kinds into the street. It was one of the hazards of medieval life, even though householders could be fined for doing this.

Viking York

When the Roman legion left York *c*. 400 CE, the aqueducts, sewers and baths were abandoned. Few people lived there during the Saxon period in the fifth to eighth centuries, but the city grew rapidly in the ninth and tenth centuries, when it became a great trading center. It filled with Viking settlers from Scandinavia and was known by its Viking name, "Jorvik."

Jorvik was a filthy place. Pigs, chickens and other animals roamed the streets. Rats and mice and hawks and falcons scavenged amidst the rubbish. The Vikings made wicker-lined pits to hold rubbish, but there was no one who could order people to use these pits or have them emptied regularly. Archaeologists have found that the streets were full of rotting fish bones, animal dung,

A street in the Viking city of Jorvik, reconstructed in the Jorvik museum.

food waste and even human faeces. Local people collected water for drinking and cooking from the river or from storage pits, which were often next to the cesspits that people used as toilets.

York in the later Middle Ages

By the 1200s, however, life in York was returning to Roman standards of cleanliness. Many houses had stone foundations and some were built entirely of stone. Cesspits were lined with brick or stone and so were less likely to leak into drinking water supplies. Sewers had been built to take waste away from the city. The biggest problem for York and other medieval towns was keeping the streets clean when they were constantly full of horses and other animals. Edward III was very critical of York (see panel), but he may have been exaggerating to make sure York was cleaned up before he arrived for a meeting of Parliament!

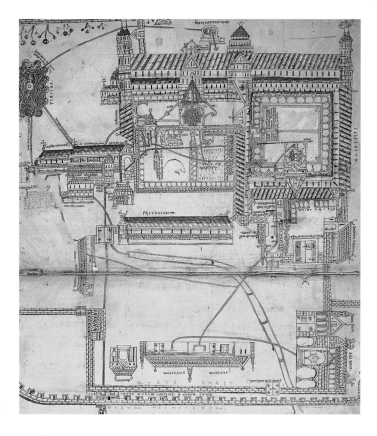

A plan of the complex water system at Canterbury Abbey, drawn by the engineer who designed it. Wealthy abbeys could afford the best facilities. The abbey of St. Mary's in York also had a stone sewer and piping system that brought in fresh water.

The abominable smell!

In 1332 Edward III wrote to the city of York:

The King detests the abominable smell abounding in the city, more than in any other city of the realm, from dung and manure and other filth and dirt, which fills and obstructs the streets. Wishing to protect the health of the inhabitants and those coming to the parliament to be held in the city, orders the city to cause all the streets and lanes to be cleansed and to be kept clean.

The streets of London

The evidence from York tells us that at different times throughout its history it was dirtier, and therefore more unhealthy, than at other times. The records of the city of London help us build up an even more complex and interesting picture of how a great city dealt with dangers to health. By 1400, London had a population close to 50,000, many of whom kept animals, such as horses for transport or cattle for meat and milk. Others regularly brought herds of cattle, sheep and even geese to the city to be butchered for food. The large number of people and animals meant that keeping the streets clean was immensely difficult.

One regular problem was the waste left after animals were butchered. Butchers were ordered to load waste on to boats and dump it in the river so the tide could carry it out to sea. Anyone throwing blood or other waste into the streets was fined. The city dealt with the problem of dirt in the streets by employing at least twelve teams of

The River Thames flows past the Tower of London, shown in a fifteenth-century illustration. Rivers were used as dumping grounds for waste. Butchers were expected to row out into the middle of the river to dump skin and bones after butchering animals, but they were often tempted to break the law by dropping waste in the streets or on the river bank.

rakers, who had to clear the streets of dung and cart it off to the countryside where it was usually spread on the fields as fertilizer.

Toilets

Toilets and sewers were essential. By the 1380s there were thirteen common privies, which had to be regularly cleaned out. One was built over the Thames, but that meant that the river water was likely to become infected. Houseowners living next to streams also adopted the bad habit of building their own toilets near the stream water, which was used by others for cooking and drinking. Whatever rules or laws the city leaders instigated, people found a way around the regulations.

Richard Whittington, who became Lord Mayor of London three times. He left money in his will to build a latrine that would provide 128 seats for the people of London – 64 seats were for men and 64 for women. The latrine was built next to the Thames; the river water flushed it out at high tide.

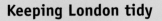

Keeping London tidy

In fourteenth-century London, the fine for throwing litter into the street was two shillings—approximately two weeks' wages for a farm laborer—and anyone who let garbage build up outside his house was fined four shillings. People also were arrested for throwing garbage in the street and, by 1414, informers were being paid for identifying anyone who dropped garbage. Clearly people did care about keeping their streets clean. In 1307 two citizens saw Thomas Scott urinating in the street instead of using the public privy (public toilets). They stopped to complain, but he attacked them for interfering. Scott was arrested and fined for the assault.

Did they link dirt and disease?

There is plenty of evidence that people did make a link between dirt and disease, even if they had no scientific understanding of what the link was. For example, in April 1349, at the height of the Black Death, Edward III wrote to the Mayor of London ordering him to have the "filth lying in the streets removed with all speed to places far distant". The King went on to demand that the city be cleansed "from all odors so that no great mortality may arise from such smells …the filth from the houses is infecting the air, endangering people through the contagious sickness which is increasing daily." Clearly there was a belief that dirt poisoned the air and the poisoned air then made people ill. The evidence in the panel also shows that people were more concerned about keeping London clean at the time of the Black Death.

Fifteenth-century houses like this one were solidly built, often by professional carpenters, and had iron locks and door-hinges. People swept them thoroughly to keep them clean and archaeologists have found the hollows made by the brooms. This house can be seen at the Weald and Downland Museum in southern England.

Londoners also tried to keep their water supplies away from cesspits (where waste water or sewage was stored) and latrines. People in private houses built latrines that were lined with stone, tiles and cement to prevent leaks. The city's regulations said that stone-walled cesspools had to be built at least 2 1/2 feet away from a neighbor's land and earth-lined cesspits over 3 1/4 feet away. However, this still meant that cesspits were liable to leak into wells containing water.

Overall, the city authorities did their best to keep the city clean. Far from not caring about the state of the streets, they worked hard to keep them as clean as possible, but it was a losing battle in the days when animals thronged the streets.

A water-seller, illustrated in the fourteenth-century English manuscript, the "Luttrell Psalter." Without pipes to bring water into houses, people had to carry water, which was surprisingly heavy, along streets or up staircases. The water-seller made this task a little easier.

The impact of the Black Death

The records of the City of London show that there was far more concern about street cleaning and butchers' waste in the years after the Black Death struck in 1348.

	Entries in records about street cleaning	Complaints about butchers' waste
1300–1350	16	2
1350–1400	65	21
1400–1450	24	3
1450–1500	9	4

Chapter 6

Medicine beyond Europe

The Islamic world

The religion of Islam was founded by the prophet Muhammad (570–632 CE). In the following centuries it spread through Arabia, across north Africa and into Spain and also eastwards into what is known today as Iraq, Iran and central Asia. Cities such as Cordoba and Seville were the links between Christian Europe and Islamic north Africa and Arabia.

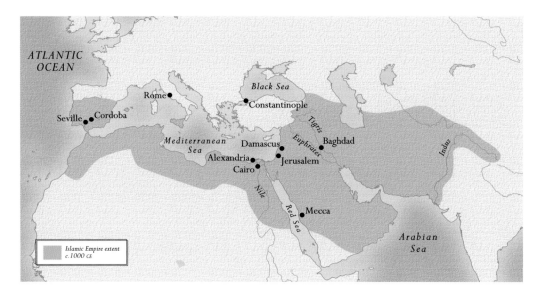

Pre-Islamic medicine in Arabia had been much like medicine in other early societies. Healers used plants and herbs in their remedies, carried out simple surgery and believed that spirits called the "jinn" (the plural "jinni" gives us the word "genie") caused some illnesses. Arab-Islamic medicine took a great step forward during the reign of Harun al-Rashid (786–809), one of the richest and greatest rulers of the Islamic empire, when many ancient medical texts were translated from Greek and Latin into Arabic. This was a period of great wealth, when rulers believed it was important to develop education and not use all their money on warfare. The

This map shows the extent of the Islamic empire c. 1000 CE.

city of Baghdad was the main center for gathering and translating medical texts. The key individual was Hunayn ibn Ishaq (808–873), who was known in Europe as "Johannitus." He and his followers translated 129 of Galen's works into Arabic.

So many texts were translated that students and doctors soon wanted books that summarized all this medical knowledge. Some of the greatest Islamic doctors produced multi-volume medical encyclopaedias that preserved and organized medical knowledge with great thoroughness. One of the first was al-Razi (865–925), who wrote around 200 texts. One of his sayings was "…he who studies the works of the Ancients, gains the experience of their labor as if he had himself lived thousands of years." However, like other Islamic scholars he did not just accept the words of Galen and others. He admired Galen but said that doctors needed to question all medical writings and think for themselves. He declared "all that is written in books is worth much less than the experience of a wise doctor."

An Arab doctor takes the patient's pulse as part of his careful observation and diagnosis of an illness.

Al-Razi, measles and smallpox

Muhammad ibn Zakariya al-Razi was known in Europe as "Rhazes." Using his experience and powers of observation, he explained the difference between smallpox and measles. Until his time, all infections with rashes had been classed as one illness. Al-Razi carefully noted the differences between such illnesses, writing:

…the physical signs of measles are nearly the same as those of smallpox but nausea and inflammation are more severe, though the pains in the back are less. The rash of measles usually appears at once, but the rash of smallpox spot after spot.

The "Galen of Islam"

The books of al-Razi became well known in Europe, but even he was not as famous as Ibn Sina. Among his many books, Ibn Sina wrote *The Canon* – an encyclopaedia of all medical knowledge, including the work of the Greeks but adding his own ideas and methods. For the rest of the Middle Ages, this book was

A European image of Ibn Sina, taken from a book printed in Venice in Italy. He is pictured as a professor dictating to a student.

The wild career of Ibn Sina

Abdallah ibn Sina (980–1037) was the son of a Persian tax collector. It was said that he could recite the whole of the *Qur'an*, the holy book of Islam, at the age of ten and was practising medicine by the time he was sixteen. Like other Islamic doctors he was not just interested in medicine but studied science, philosophy and many other subjects. He also travelled a great deal in search of knowledge and, it seems, adventure. In his autobiography he said that he had written his books while on military campaigns, while drunk and even in prison!

thought of as the most important medical book of all, not only in the Islamic world but in Europe too, where Ibn Sina became known as the "Galen of Islam."

New ideas

Although the writings of Al-Razi and Ibn Sina became famous, other Arab doctors were still prepared to question and criticize their work. This critical attitude meant that Arab medicine developed at a faster rate than medicine in western Europe, where doctors were still reluctant to question the writings of Galen. One tantalizing example is the work of Ibn al-Nafis (1200–1288), who studied at the hospital in Damascus and wrote many books giving his views on the works of Ibn Sina and other writers.

One of the topics that al-Nafis investigated was the anatomy of the heart. Galen had said that the blood moves from one side of the heart to the other through invisible channels, but al-Nafis used his own observations to say that Galen must be wrong. These "invisible" channels could not be seen because they did not exist. He suggested that the blood moved from the heart to the lungs and then back to the heart; it circulated around the body. This idea was correct, but nobody built on his work and it was to be another 300 years before the circulation of the blood was widely understood.

This Turkish illustration from the fifteenth century shows a patient being held just before surgery. The leading Arab writer on surgery was al-Zahrawi (936–1013), known as "Albucasis" in Europe, where his writings were also widely read. His books included illustrations of surgical instruments, some of which he had designed himself to improve on existing instruments.

ومنه أسود فالأبيض هو الشميط بالبربيه وهو البنكران

Herbal remedies were just as common in Islamic medicine as in Europe. This is a page from an Arabic herbal, giving a clear illustration of the plant so mistakes would be less likely!

Drugs and hospitals in Arab medicine

The Roman writer Dioscorides had listed around 1,000 remedies made from plants, minerals and animal parts. Islamic doctors prepared an even greater number of remedies, developing new drugs, such as senna, laudanum, camphor, and myrrh, which all became widely used in Europe. The word "drug" itself comes from Arabic, as do sugar, syrup, alcohol (originally a powder taken as a remedy) and alkali. The Arab world also was famous for its hospitals. The first was founded in Baghdad around 805, and by the twelfth century every large town in the Islamic empire had a hospital. One of the most famous was built at Cairo in 1283, dedicated to all who needed care. It had wards for mental and physical problems, an operating room, a pharmacy, a library, lecture rooms, and a Christian chapel as well as a mosque.

Moses Maimonides (1135-1204)

The Jews also belonged to the Levantine world, with Maimonides, who spent most of his life in Cairo, the leading Jewish medical writer of the medieval period. A scholar of philosophy, theology and medicine, Maimonides was appointed court physician to Saladin, sultan of Egypt and Syria in 1174. He produced ten medical works, ranging from writings on Hippocrates and Galen to short practical pieces on ailments such as constipation and asthma, all of which earned him great respect, both in Europe and the Islamic world.

Chinese medicine

The earliest Chinese medical books date from the time of the Han dynasty (206 BCE to 220 CE). This was a time of peace and prosperity when the emperor and his government valued education and learning. Chinese doctors believed that *qi* (pronounced "chi") was the vital energy or life force that flowed around the body. To stay healthy, a person had to keep *qi* flowing and also had to keep the forces of Yin and Yang in balance. They believed that Yin and Yang were in everything around us, but were opposites – light and dark, cold and hot, winter and summer. A healthy person had to spend time in both the sun and shade, resting and being active. Therefore a doctor's task was to advise his patients how to keep the forces of Yin and Yang in balance in order to remain healthy. If patients became sick, the doctor's job was to find a way to restore their balance.

The symbols of Yin and Yang, which were central to Chinese medical beliefs.

Yin and Yang

This quotation is from the *Yellow Emperor's Manual of Medicine* written around 400 BCE:

On the outside of the body there is Yang, and inside there is Yin. The liver, heart, spleen, lungs and kidneys are Yin and the five hollow organs, gall bladder, stomach, lower intestines and bladder are all Yang. The diseases of spring are located within the Yin areas of the body and the diseases of autumn in the Yang areas. We must know the locations of these diseases for the purpose of acupuncture [see page 52].

Chinese treatments

A Chinese doctor advised his patients how to keep themselves healthy. A good diet, exercise, meditation and the use of herbs were all ways of keeping the qi flowing and maintaining the balance of Yin and Yang. If a patient became ill, then a doctor took a detailed medical history of the patient before looking in more detail at his temperature, complexion, appetite and digestion. Taking the patient's pulse was the most vital part of the examination because this gave information about the flow of qi.

The most common treatment, as in other societies, was the use of drugs, taken as pills, powders or syrups made up from very precise amounts of the ingredients by the doctor or a pharmacist. However, Chinese medicine also used methods that were not found elsewhere, notably acupuncture. Acupuncture involves inserting long, fine metal needles into very precise points in the body, called "pressure points."

Surgery was not part of Chinese everyday medicine, but it was needed on the battlefield. Here, the surgeon, Hua Tuo, is operating on the arm of General Kuan Yun.

The acupuncture points lie on invisible lines called "meridians," which run from head to toe. Specific points on the meridians relate to particular ailments and parts of the body. The needles may be inserted gently or with force, depending on the diagnosis and then may be twirled and vibrated. The purpose is to restore the body's qi and so make the patient well. Another treatment was moxibustion, which involved burning small cones or pellets made up from herbs at specific points on the body, again to stimulate and restore the qi. Acupuncture and moxibustion continued to be used for many centuries and are still widely used today, even in the West, as "alternative" medical approaches.

Of course, not all healers were physicians who made careful diagnoses and used acupuncture. The vast majority of healers were not qualified in any way, except through experience. Physicians believed that women were too ignorant to play any proper role in medicine, but women were regarded as the best midwives.

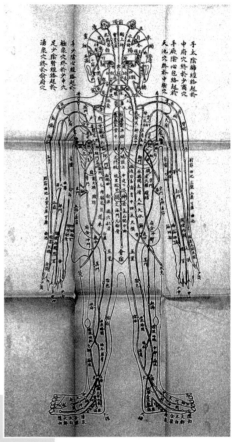

A chart showing the acupuncture points in the body.

A Chinese examination

Students of acupuncture tested their skills on a model of a man. The model contained tiny pinholes at all the acupuncture points. However, when it was time for an examination, the model was filled with water and then the pinholes were covered with wax so that the students could not see them. The students were expected to know the position of the acupuncture points so accurately that they could locate them and insert the needles even though they were not immediately visible. If they found the points accurately, then they pierced the wax and the water spurted out. If there was no water, they failed the test!

Ayurvedic medicine

The major system of Indian medicine was known as "ayurvedic" medicine, from the words *ayus* meaning longevity and *veda* meaning knowledge. Ayurvedic medicine was based on the knowledge needed to live a long, healthy life. The main books describing this type of medicine date from the second and third centuries CE and are called the *Caraka Samhita* (Caraka's Compendium) and the *Susruta Samhita* (Susruta's Compendium). They are lengthy encyclopaedias of medical knowledge, covering drugs, how to examine patients and the symptoms and treatment of illnesses. At the heart of the system was the belief that health depended on keeping three humors in the body (wind, bile and phlegm) in balance.

Doctors were required to take an Oath of Initiation, swearing to treat all information about the patient as confidential and to do everything possible to help their

An Indian doctor taking the pulse of a patient. From the thirteenth century onwards, taking the pulse was the most important means of diagnosing an illness.

patients. The *Caraka Samhita* described a good doctor as "courteous, wise, self-disciplined and a master of his subject. He is alike a guru, a master of life itself." Despite the existence of books, doctors learned by heart the major texts so that they could remember the symptoms and treatments when examining a patient, rather than having to leave the patient to consult a book. From the eleventh century, one of the main means of diagnosis was examining the patient's urine, just as it was in Europe. Astrology also was important, as different parts of the body were said to be linked to the planets and the constellations of stars.

Natural remedies

Indian doctors used a wide range of remedies made up from plants, minerals and animal parts and products, such as the blood, milk, fat and dung of a wide range of animals, from snakes to camels and elephants. As the cow was a holy animal in the Hindu religion, its products were seen as purifying. Therefore cow dung was used to treat infections and cow urine was an ingredient in many recipes.

Indian surgeons reconstructed a nose by grafting skin from the face. The drawings at the bottom instruct surgeons how to cut skin from the forehead to remodel the nose.

An Indian miracle

In 1793 two English surgeons watched an operation that gave an indication of the kinds of surgery used in India centuries earlier. A man called Cowasjee, who worked for the English army, was captured by an Indian ruler and had one hand and his nose cut off for treachery. Indian surgeons repaired his nose by grafting skin from his face and using it to reconstruct his nose. The English surgeons were so amazed by the success of the operation that they sent a description of the operation back to Britain where the method was copied.

Chapter 7

How successful was medieval medicine?

Healers and their treatments

In the Middle Ages the kind of healer you visited depended on how much money you had and how desperately ill you were. Often wives and mothers treated the vast majority of illnesses. If their cures did not work, then they could visit the local market place and spend a few pennies on a travelling salesman's cure, or they could go to church and pray. University-trained physicians visited the rich at home; they had read the works of the great Greek, Roman and Arab doctors and might even have watched a dissection during their training.

The treatments offered by these healers did help with some health problems. Physicians gave good advice on taking exercise and eating a good diet. They also prescribed herbs. The herbal remedies used by all kinds of healers contained ingredients such as plantain and honey, which acted against infections. Surgeons carried out useful basic surgery developed through frequent practice.

Chaucer's physician

In the late fourteenth century, Geoffrey Chaucer wrote *The Canterbury Tales*, in which a group of pilgrims riding to Canterbury take turns telling stories. Chaucer created realistic characters that would amuse his readers. The physician knew the names of all the famous doctors but "loved he gold exceeding all."

Well read was he in Asculapius,
And Dioscorides, and in Rufus,
Hippocrates, and Hali, and Galen,
Serapion, Rhazes, and Avicen ...

An illustration from c. 1400 of the physician described by Geoffrey Chaucer in *The Canterbury Tales*. He is checking a patient's urine, one of the commonest ways to diagnose an illness.

A fifteenth-century illustration showing the bodies of dead children. Such scenes were very common because babies and young children were particularly vulnerable to infections.

Life expectancy

There was no improvement in the length of people's lives during the Middle Ages. Approximately 20 per cent of babies still died before their first birthday. Giving birth was just as dangerous for mothers, who were in danger from catching infections as well as from problems during the birth itself. Only a minority of people lived past the age of 45, but there still were elderly people, especially among the wealthier classes. Good food and less work meant that bishops and noblemen and women could expect to live past 60, with some living even longer. Evidence from skeletons shows the average height of men and women respectively to have been 5 feet 6 inches and 5 feet 2 inches, figures that are very similar to all other periods up to the late twentieth century.

A university lecturer and his students, from a manuscript dated *c.* 1300 containing the texts of Hippocrates and notes by Galen. They were still the most widely read medical writers.

The limits of medical knowledge

Medieval healers dealt effectively with some ailments but could not prevent epidemics such as the Black Death or tackle many other problems that are dealt with quite easily today. The two most important reasons for this were that people continued to believe in super-natural explanations and the Church opposed medical experiments and supported traditional theories. The most advanced explanation for illness they had was the one put forward by Hippocrates and Galen—that people became ill when the humors in their bodies were out of balance. While they had made simple connections between dirt and disease, they still did not know about bacteria as the cause of infections.

Making improvements

Doctors would not be able to make major improvements in treatments and public health until they made new discoveries. This was extremely difficult in the Middle Ages. The Christian Church controlled education and did not encourage scholars to seek new ideas or to experiment. The Church believed that Galen had said all there was to be said about medicine and that later doctors should do their best to copy Galen, not to challenge him.

However, by the fourteenth century, ideas were changing. More dissections were carried out, increasing anatomical knowledge. Ibn Sina and other Arab scholars had shown that Galen could be questioned. Just as significantly, the survivors of the Black Death became wealthier, with more resources and land shared among fewer people. Consequently, while the plague was a terrible disaster, one result was that people could spend more money on educating their children. As education improved, scholars became more confident and more willing to question old ideas. Printing developed, which revolutionized communications and the spread of medical ideas. Indeed, some very important medical developments in anatomy and surgery were just around the corner.

Medieval physicians discussing treatments and theories, from a fifteenth-century Italian manuscript. By then, physicians were more willing to challenge old ideas.

Astronomy and the Humors

In *The Canterbury Tales*, Chaucer described the physician's methods of diagnosing illness:

With us there was a doctor of physic;
In all this world was none like him to pick
For talk of medicine and surgery;
For he was grounded in astronomy.
He often kept a patient from the pall
By horoscopes and magic natural ...
He knew the cause of every malady,
Were it of hot or cold, of moist or dry,
And where engendered, and of what humour ...

Glossary

Alkali a soluble mineral salt

Anaesthetic a drug that induces pain relief, used mostly in preparation for surgery, sometimes making the person unconscious

Anatomy the study of the structure of the human body

Apothecary a pharmacist or chemist in the Middle Ages who prepared and sold drugs and medicines

Aqueduct a bridge carrying water along a pipeline

Archaeologist someone who studies the past primarily through artifacts, such as buildings, pottery, jewelry or even human remains

Arteries the blood vessels that carry blood away from the heart

Astrology the study of the stars and planets and how they might influence people's lives

Barbarians the peoples who lived outside the Roman Empire and were regarded as uncivilized by the Romans

Barber-surgeon a surgeon of lower status who often combined being a barber with minor surgery, such as cutting out bladder stones, or lancing boils.

Benedictines monks who followed St. Benedict's (*c.* 480–*c.* 547) rules for living in a monastery

Bile a fluid produced by the body that aids the digestion of fats

Blood transfusion the transference of blood from a healthy individual to one with a disease or a condition which requires blood

Cataract a growth on the eye that obscures vision

Cauterize the medical procedure of sealing an open wound to stop bleeding by using a hot piece of iron to burn the flesh around the wound

Cesspit a place for collecting and storing sewage

Commonplace book a scrapbook of interesting or useful information

Contagious a disease that can be passed from one person to another

Crusades the attempts by Christian soldiers during the Middle Ages to take back Jerusalem and the Holy Land from Islamic rule; Jerusalem was a holy city for Christians and Muslims

Dissection the cutting up and scientific examination of the human body

Dysentery a severe illness causing frequent, fluid bowel movements

Epidemic a disease affecting a large number of people at once

Epilepsy a disease of the nervous system causing convulsions and loss of consciousness

Famine a severe shortage of food leading to starvation

Gall bladder the sac or pouch in the body that holds the body's bile

Grafting taking body tissue from one part of the body to a different part; tissues can even be transferred from one person to another

Hemlock a poisonous plant and the drug obtained from the plant, sometimes used as an anaesthetic

Herbal medicines medicines made from plants

Immunity protection against a disease

Infirmary a hospital

Inflammation the reaction of living tissue to injury or infection, characterized by heat, swelling, pain and redness

Kidneys the organs that filter the blood to clean it; the kidneys excrete waste and excess water as urine

Leprosy an infection that causes severe damage to the nerves and skin, eventually leading to death

Levant the countries bordering on the eastern Mediterranean

Liver the organ that acts as the body's chemical factory, regulating the levels of the various chemicals in the blood

Mandrake a poisonous plant and the drug obtained from the plant, sometimes used as an anaesthetic

Midwife a person who assists at a birth

Noisome disgusting

Opium a drug obtained from the poppy plant that makes people sleepy; it has been used as an anaesthetic

Parchment the skin of animals (such as sheep or calves) on which people can write

Pestilence the name used by people in the fourteenth century for the Black Death (bubonic plague)

Pharmacy the study and making of drugs for use as medicines

Physic medicine

Physician a university-trained doctor

Pores minute openings through the skin

Purge to cleanse the body by taking drugs to make people vomit or empty their bowels

Pus a pale yellow or green fluid found where there is an infection

Sinew a tendon that joins a muscle to a bone

Smallpox a disease similar to influenza that leads to a severe rash and blisters; it affected humans for many centuries but became much more dangerous from the eighteenth century onwards, killing 40 per cent of sufferers; it is now extinct

Spleen the organ that removes worn-out blood cells and fights infections

Stupor a state of unconsciousness

Trepanning (also trephining) drilling a hole into the skull for medical reasons in order to relieve pressure on the brain

Tumor a swelling caused by cells reproducing at an abnormal rate

Veins blood vessels that carry blood towards the heart

Timeline

Events	Dates CE	People
c. 400–500 Collapse of the Roman Empire in western Europe		
	500	
		Lifetime of the prophet Muhammad 570–632, founder of Islam
805 Foundation of hospital at Baghdad		Hunayn ibn Ishaq died 873, translator of many of Galen's books into Arabic
c. 900 Anglo-Saxon medical book known as *Bald's Leechbook* written		Al Razi (865–925), author of around 200 medical texts; known as "Rhazes" in the West
		Al Zahrawi (936–1013), leading Arab writer on surgery; known as "Albucasis" in the West
		Ibn Sinna (980–1037), leading Arab medical writer and author of *The Canon*; known as "Avicenna" in the West
	1000	
c. 1100 Foundation of medical school at Salerno in Italy		Hildegard of Bingen (1098–1179), author of medical books including herbals
1123 Foundation of St Bartholomew's hospital, London		
Foundation of universities: Paris 1110, Bologna 1158, Oxford 1167, Montpellier 1181, Cambridge 1209, Padua 1222		Roger of Salerno, author of textbook on surgery c. 1180
		Ibn al Nafis (1200–1288), Arab medical scholar, surgeon and writer
		Theodoric of Lucca (1205–1296), surgeon and writer
		Henri de Mondeville (c. 1260–c. 1320), surgeon and writer
c. 1315 Dissection became a compulsory part of the medical curriculum for the first time at the University of Bologna		Guy de Chauliac, surgeon and medical author, c. 1298–1368
1348 The first outbreaks of the Black Death in Europe		
1453 Fall of Constantinople		
	1500	

Further information

Books

Blood and Guts, A Short History of Medicine,
Roy Porter, W. W. Norton & Co., 2003
An entertaining, up-to-date history for older readers.

The Illustrated History of Surgery,
Knut Haeger, Harold Starke, 2000

Terry Jones' Medieval Lives,
Terry Jones, BBC Books, 2004

Medicine and Society in Later Medieval England,
Carole Rawcliffe, Sutton Pub. Ltd, 1998

The Black Death,
Philip Ziegler, Sutton Pub. Ltd., 1997
Well-illustrated, clear histories for older readers.

The Measly Middle Age,(Horrible Histories),
Terry Deary, Scholastic, 1998
Entertaining, funny and informative.

Medieval Realms: Daily Life,
P. Chrisp, Hodder Wayland, 2004

Life in a Medieval Abbey,
T. McAleavy, Enchanted Lion Books, 2003

Life in a Medieval Castle,
T. McAleavy, Enchanted Lion Books, 2003

Medieval Realms: Death and Disease,
A. Woolf, Lucent, 2004

The Middle Ages: An Illustrated History,
B. Hanawalt, Oxford University Press, 1998

How Would You Survive the Middle Ages,
F. MacDonald, Franklin Watts, Inc., 1997
A selection of well-illustrated information books on daily life and other key aspects of medieval history.

Websites

www.bbc.co.uk
Search for "middle ages" here to arrive at a good list of sites on medieval times, history and health.

www.medhist.ac.uk
A guide to websites on the history of medicine, chiefly aimed at an academic audience.

www.cwru.edu/artsci/dittrick/links.htm
Dittrick Medical History Center at Case Western Reserve University provides useful links, including medical museums in the USA and overseas and thematic virtual museums.

www.learner.org/exhibits/middleages/morhealt.html
Information of medieval medicine with linksto to other medieval sites.

www.intermaggie.com/med
An interesting and informative site on many aspects of medieval medicine.

www.georgetown.edu/labyrinth
The best clearinghouse for medieval sites on the Internet.

www.mnsu.edu/emuseum/history/middleages
A site for exploring medieval life and culture.

www.metmuseum.org/Works_of_Art/collection.asp
Site for the Cloisters and the Metropolitan Museum's medieval collections.

Places to visit

The Cloisters, New York City
www.metmuseum.org
A branch of the Metropolitan Museum of Art devoted to the art and architecture of medieval Europe. Includes the famous unicorn tapestries and a medieval herb garden

The Metropolitan Museum of Art, New York City
www.metmuseum.org
Displays many medieval objects, including an excellent collection of arms and armor.

Mutter Museum, Philadelphia, PA
www.collphyphil.org/muttpgl.shtml
Collections include over 10,000 medical instruments, apparati, and specimens, primarily dating between 1750 and the present.

International Museum of Surgical Science, Chicago, IL
www.imss.org
Devoted to the history of surgery. .

California Science Center, Los Angeles, CA
www.casciencectr.org
The West Coast's largest hands-on science center.

St. Louis Science Center, St. Louis, MO
www.slsc.org
Home to a significant medical artifact collection, originally belonging to the St. Louis Medical Society.

Index